Soldier of the Cross

BOB KELEHER

SOLDIER OF THE CROSS

iUniverse books may be ordered through booksellers or by contacting:

iUniverse
1663 Liberty Drive
Bloomington, IN 47403
www.iuniverse.com
844-349-9409

Because of the dynamic nature of the Internet, any web addresses or links contained in this book may have changed since publication and may no longer be valid. The views expressed in this work are solely those of the author and do not necessarily reflect the views of the publisher, and the publisher hereby disclaims any responsibility for them.

Any people depicted in stock imagery provided by Getty Images are models, and such images are being used for illustrative purposes only. Certain stock imagery © Getty Images.

ISBN: 978-1-6632-6524-1 (sc)
ISBN: 978-1-6632-6525-8 (e)

Print information available on the last page.

iUniverse rev. date: 07/23/2024

Dedicated

To Ralph, who turned my life around
To Don, who told me "Write that down"
To Geezer, who loved me like a mother
And to Cal, who loved me like no other

Contents

Always

When the morning chill fills your body,
When the sun's prying your not ready eyes,
May your faith in continuing be steadfast
With the one who with you lies ...
I will always love you.

We started in life and loving together
In a spirit no storm's been able to shake.
We've raised not just ourselves but also ours
Neglecting the cost but not what's at stake ...
I will always remember.

When your sunsets become all too lonely
And my response to your call is long delays,
Let no bitterness steal your contentment
For then as now, in so many ways ...
I will always be there.

Summer

Nothing to me marks the full sway of Summer
As the bouncy fresh step of a shapely young mother,
Strolling gently their strollers with new lads or lasses
Swaying back and forth, up and down, like the seasons long grasses.
Nothing could spoil this picture of young mom, lass (or lad)
Unless she's out walking along with the dad.

The Star

I can't imagine a single soul having sound reason
For disliking the jingle bell, snowflake-covered season.
But if he were swimming in eggnog, there's one man I know
That couldn't warm his heart by the hearth in the fire's amber glow.
I'm sure he took joy in the miracle born in the hay,
But the event's celebration reminds him of the one day
To bring home a fresh pine tree (from who knows how far?)
And the annual Olympic event of placing the star.

To get the prickly pine to inside was a sight.
Then sawing it down to its eleven foot height.
Next cutting limbs from the back and boring holes in the trunk
To restick limbs in so it looks right from up front.
Soon this evergreen would sparkle like the moon on the ocean
And to his bitter regret the tree had the same motion.
He sat sweating, half-covered in the pine's sticky tar,
And thought he heard "Taps" playing as Grandma unpacked the
star.

With the anticipation of the world on the first Christmas night
He plugged the star in the wall and prayed it would light.
It didn't. So again he conducts his electrical rape
Pop it open and unravel miles of old friction tape,
Never thinking of unplugging before he's begun
And caught the smell of fried pine pitch (his fingers, well done).
He wanted to remedy burnt fingers down at Moe Roane's bar
But knew he'd only come back, to get back to the star.

He finally got the five points lit but his heart got even sadder
As now was the time to climb the wobbly six-foot stepladder.
We watched him gallop the ladder that he was astride,

He got the star in position but saw the plug's on the far side.
So he got up on his tip-toes, that's when he called the Lord's Name
And started flapping arms like drunk angels in a wild hurricane.
As his hand jammed in the radiator he knew he'd reached too far.
His belly landed in the tree stand, and on his back lay the star.

The doctor was summoned from the big house next door,
To revive the poor Santa in the tree on the floor.
"Tell her my thumb is not broke, Doc.". "No, you tell her, Jack.'
While doc grabbed the appendage and pulled it straight back.
By the time Dad came to the hard cast was in place,
Broken light bulbs and needles were removed from his face.
Mom got him a beer and I brought in a cigar,
And we hoisted the tree up <u>after</u> aligning the star.

Mom put on the old 78s and we all joined in
With the familiar crooning's of Bing written by Irv Berlin.
By suppertime we saw snowflakes dancing about.
All he saw was the tree topping, one light had burnt out.
None of us knew this would be the last one that we had,
Of the Christmases we'd share with the star and with Dad.
But it will remain a symbol of bringing kings from afar,
And bringing family closer together, beneath the star.

Courage

Fear is the lock that binds the spirit and imprisons you and me.
Cowardice and avoidance extend the term,
Courage is the key.

Cowering in the darkness and crying aloud never made an issue right.
Hiding the truth makes you small and alone,
Courage is the light.

Looking the other way, not getting involved, may expand your lifeline length
But weak in values and afraid to live,
Courage is the strength.

So do not wait or hesitate to open new and challenging doors,
And whether it's popular or not, just take your stand,
Courage is then yours.

Epitaphs

What becomes of us when we're left in the dust?
When we don't share a tear or a laugh.
As we lie alone, our head holding a stone,
Our life's work phrased in brief epitaph.

Whether it's heaven or hell, will carved words treat us well,
When we have the green grass for a roof?
For all who stop there, to gaze, read or stare
Will our reflected result be the truth?

Shouldn't we chisel our own for this garden of stone,
Instead of leaving it up to some stranger?
So, at long, long last when we become past,
Our eternal fact's not in danger.

With the others underground, and their tombstones around,
We're blending our issues with theirs.
Wouldn't we be delighted (being oh, so farsighted)
To make folks wonder if we went up or downstairs?

Soldier's Prayer

Dear God, I serve You with all I've got,
If in peril I forget You, forget me not.
Let me strike my enemies with strange respect
And let no man of mine die from my neglect.
If the decision to fight falls to me alone
Lead us to success and safely home.
In all I say and do, please be my guide,
When others turn and run, stay by my side.
I'll pray to You each night before going to bed,
And trust You'll keep Your symbol from standing above my head.

320

Footsteps echoing in empty halls
Of a house, no longer a home
Gone is the furniture, the pictures off walls
Even the fire screen from the hearthstone.
The torn shades are pulled, the glass looks black,
And lack of heat makes the body cold.
In leaving now I can never come back,
It's no longer "For Sale," it's sold

Solitude is a friend when memory needs to be strong
Because no one else can ever have yours.
Loneliness, a disease, it's duration is long
And I've yet to find any cures.
The value of youth dropped before the price of this place
If my truth would ever be told,
As I watched relatives carried out with ashen face
Before anyone had turned old.

Time doesn't wash the haunting effect
Of the bittersweet of years gone by.
Nor can it change my knowledge of my lack of respect
When I should have been saying good-bye.
Chilling thoughts of their partings accompany me now
In the rooms where we once hugged goodnight.
As if my ongoing pain of each argument and row
Could at this last hour make it right.

Yes, there are ghosts, and I'll carry them out the door
To look over my shoulder forever.
I'm sure that they haunt the other four
Although they seem to talk of it, never.
This ill place took a child away from its mother
And before that made that child into a widow.
I'll take a rock from the garden as a memento.
No, I'll just throw it through a window.

Rhyme in Ranks

So you think it strange that soldiers like me
Can set their thoughts to poetry?
You issue astonished and inquiring looks
To those learning through living, in lieu of books.
Well *we* don't learn as much from the dead as we do from the dying,
Too young to know causes or the truths underlying.

If you'd had the waiting time we did, search our hearts,
On the good friend at breakfast by dinner, in parts.
You gut yourself like a fish (and scrape emotions out, too)
Then, when you can afford to return them, they come back to
you new.
It's like the air after a storm, it's ever so clear.
And you repeat the procedure each time you face fear.

That's why many a soldier acquires The Stare.
After removal, and review all, you see the beast there.
Soon finding the greatest fight is the one that's inside,
The spoils being clearer focus and perhaps, thicker hide.
But no matter how fresh, or over years grown near dormant,
We seek only to teach others, what we know as important.

•

Vic

Your accomplishments are many times expressed,
In a long and flowery tone.

But the greatest gifts to humanity,
Are the ones that go unknown.

The Day that Freedom Cried
[The fall of Saigon]

The awful scenes they showed, but you couldn't turn away,
It wasn't green fields and grass huts they brought back for us today.
Now it's city blocks and buildings and rescues from their tops.
We took our risks and our best shot, now we took it in the chops.

Our friends scrambled up the fences and we butt-stroked them down,
As "unfriendly" folks were rolling in the outskirts of the town.
Tear gas filled the young lungs making children cry and cough.
This time when the smoke has cleared away we won't be there to dust them off.

The fecal material has finally hit the rotary device.
We give their country back to them full of broken dreams, and lice.
We've prostituted all their daughters and made smugglers of their last son,
Now let's go back and write the history to make it read like we have won.

As their eyes and arms reached up to us through the television screen,
Dad carved the roast before us wondering if the meat's too lean.
A mother crying wildly passing a baby through the gate.
Mom said "Sure makes the US look bad" as she filled another plate.

The last went whirling up and away to the safety of the sea.
The camera shot from overhead blurred momentarily.
And as I looked and squinted down, into the crowded street,
I saw my own face looking up, in disgust and in defeat.

Beneath the Shadow of the Flags

How well the country wheels and deals
In lost causes and young soldier yields.
Patriots in black bags, to go.
Only the day was new, the story's the same,
No one carrying can remember his name.
You always reap the death you sow.

And what to do with the last remains?
Send them home to organ strains.
Very few know, even less care.
Lowered down six feet to it's final stop,
The folded flag the widow drops.
But true to form, no tear falls there.

Years from now the nation will heal,
And, halfheartedly, for themselves, the bell will peal.
A rotted corpse in tattered rags.
The cold earth keeping them apart,
Warms him more than all their hearts.
Beneath the shadow of the flags.

Perhaps, someday, the corpse will tell,
How a bullet saved his soul from Hell.
Bluntly, not profound.
No priest caught his final breath,
Nor Scripture at his time of death.
To him, God was" a round".

Night

When evening falls and black surrounds,
Do you turn to others or within?
As sorrow and shadows fast abound
and the bogeyman comes drifting in.

All the joys of my day just slide away
And the smiles from my memory seeps.
The bogeyman comes in to stay
Putting tastes of steel between my teeth.

The softness on the pillow next to mine
Gently stirring in dreams of peace.
Never knowing I leave her and wander time,
Spending my nighttime with the beast.

He's been with me for years (just like a friend)
Not always seen but always there
Visiting each night until the end
Defiantly meeting my gaze with his stare.

A night will come when he'll be no more,
Knocking cold on my mind's windowpane.
Let him go find another that cannot ignore
The guilt of a survivor's brain.

Followers

Often's the time as bands step out in line
That bittersweet tears fill an eye,
As the flag is unfurled and I sit on the curb
Only to watch the parade pass me by.

Patriotic hearts will dull pride once again step aside
And let center stage go to young brothers.
Let them gain the applause in their far purer cause,
But let them not quite forget, there were others.

We lost friends, just as dear, in our mission, unclear,
And suffered conditions as rough.
We won the fights, as before, but in the end lost the war.
There and here, politically handcuffed.

So, before you leave this scene and fill fresh magazines,
Hear this echoing voice from the past.
As your president gives orders make sure his headquarters,
Are not firmly placed well up his ass.

Gone

Here he is, a star of yours,
That shines now, not so brightly.
God, come take this soul from earth
But for your sake don't take him lightly.
He's a good man, a worker, a poet, a fighter,
A knight in armor of rust.
His wish was that he, and our memory of him,
Be buried down deep in the dust.
His battles are won. His race is now done.
He's given up the last of his cares.
Just one honor more, let us nail to his door,
A sign stating that "He's moved upstairs."

The Precious Gift

We rejoiced the day you shared the news
Your family had begun.
We all celebrated when we heard
You had a little son.
We spent countless hours praying,
With folded hands, and fingers crossed.
And now we stand behind you
To support you in your loss.

Though it will not take away the pain
Or all your hurts and fears,
You've loved your child more in these weeks
Than we do, for ours, in years.
We can't imagine your emotions now
Nor count the anxious steps you've trod.
But we admire your sacrifice and courage
In giving this precious gift to God.

Rebecca

Smiles are daughters young at heart
Holding on to fluffy pets.
Tears are young girls growing up,
From dads with deep regrets.

While sons to manhood touch fatherly hearts
We rejoice to see them grown.
But a girl to a woman grips us with fear,
And feelings we've never known.

Becky, I've a love from deep inside
That's as precious as it's true.
Though years and miles may come between,
It's always here for you.

The Sexton

It's Christmas Eve in Wethersfield,
There's no one else on Main Street.
The only sound's my feet coming down
And the sign's familiar creak.

The candles were put out hours ago
(not a duty I'd ever shirk)
And no matter how I search, my time in the church
Can never be considered my work.

The first snow of winter begins to fall
Through the air so cold and still.
By the glow of streetlights on this longest of nights
I can see Cemetery Hill.

I've got the time and take the climb,
Without any feeling of loss.
With my face to the sky, and a tear in my eye,
I wish Him "Happy Birthday, Boss."

Barbie

I'm way too old for the likes of this,
If told I'd be doing so, I'd have said "hardly'"
But I opened an old box of my wife's today
And saw in it, a beautiful "Barbie."

I wanted to longingly lift the hem of her dress
To see her legs, so slender and splendid.
But I thought it too dear, and my wife was too near
So I didn't, but I'm quite sure that "Ken" did.

R.C.M.P.

Justice and the Mounties, let no man put asunder.
But what about the tall mount that rides him from down under?
Mounties chase their man through rain, darkness and snow,
Never giving due credit to the beast just below.

Did the Mountie, ever once, take a minute to thank it
Late cold nights on the trail when he steals the horse blanket?
The R.C.M.P. gets the glory, indeed,
But wouldn't have gotten the bad guy if it weren't for his steed.

That horse takes the rocks in the road and swims the redcoat through
water,
Never getting the recognition and glory he oughta.
The mare does the same hours, then while Mountie-boy sleeps,
He guards the camp all night long, catching Zs on his feet.

Day and dark he is harnessed, carrying this legend to fame,
While the redcoat's speeched and honored, the horse chomps on
his grain.
We could right this great wrong and bring abuse to a stop,
If the Mountie, just once, let the mount get on top.

A Kiss

The romantic "Saint of Valentine" is just a vicious rumor.
His timing of his holiday shows a twisted sense of humor.
Yes, a box of sweets, dine in candle glow, the table garnished with a rose,
Cannot overtake or compensate for a seasonally draining nose.

The fireplace burns cheerfully far from the circling snow,
But 'tis not enough for your dearest to don a silken gown, when it's twenty degrees below.
Her ear takes rapture from your lips blowing loving, passionate breezes.
And without much fuss, you chance to buss between earthshaking sneezes.

If you should be fortunate enough to usher her to bed,
And ignore feverish face, cold feet and eyes shot with red,
To awaken from your antihistamine dream, and not act all that stupid,
You can thank your Saint of Valentine and the plump-rumped archer, Cupid.

Marbles Exist

When did it all become less than we wanted?
Dollar signs,
Less time,
Friends leaving.

Wishes and hopes that made us happy, then.
Reality came,
Innocence left.
Memories fade.

You broke your promises to yourself.
Blame time changing,
Curse your associates.
If only now ...

Meadows are still available to walk in.
Marbles exist,
Songs wait,
Time's yours.

No one imprisons you to today
but yourself.
Your life.
Marbles exist.

Shark

Some don't like the taste of shark, I do.
Better you eat him than he eat you.

I'm God

I'm not the church, I'm not the steeple,
But without me here there'd be none of you people

I just came down to see you (Sunday morning, of course)
And I found you out playing a round out on the golf course.
So I walked to the city to talk to you all,
But you weren't in the church, you were out at the mall.
I knew I'd find you at worship, if not now then later,
But at ten you're still in bed with the Sunday newspaper.

I'd been walking for weeks and was not very pleased.
I said "This is not good," (and this is no tease).
I started gathering clouds to block the moon and the stars,
To start forty days of cold rain to wash away your new cars.

Then I heard a tune, my Me, that was a hymn!
I walked up to My house and slowly stepped in.
By accident in with Me came a cold blast of December.
"Were you brought up in a barn?"
"No, but My Son's born in one, remember?"

Love Letters

Memories so sweet and held so dear.
(Mirrors showing bitter truth)
A bag so full of yesterdays,
It won't hold one more tomorrow.

Letters in the light of day,
Cherished more close to dusk and dark.
Remembering's always a wonderful thing,
As long as no one else can see it.

Love letters are best, burned.

First Death

You're in bitter darkness,
There's no food to taste,
Body tissue and blood surround you
Inches from human waste.
Who would put you in here,
Seemingly to meet your end?
You don't know him yet?
He's your father, my friend.
He condemned you to life
In this cramped, lightless room.
No, you're not in prison,
You're just still in the womb.

What's next? ... Your mom
From cart to table is rolled.
Her legs are spread, they grab your head
And drag you out into the cold.
The masked man holds you up
Upside down, by your toes.
A damp fleshy cord
Is banging your nose.
The cord gets cut and tied
To a neat little stump,
The masked man raises his hand
And slaps down on your rump.
You let out a scream
All the others there grin.
With this welcome to life
Surprised you don't crawl right back in!

And how would I know
Of your trip from inside?
Well, shake blue hands, brother
I was right by your side.

The Procedure

My macho worlds around me crumble
A passive patient on a slab to humble.
My clothes on the floor, in a kit'n caboodle
And me in a pose that looks more like a poodle.

The jellied doctor, in being kind
Speaks of being up front about my behind.
My objections are strong but my voice gets weak
With his finger beyond my cheek to cheek.

The bright light he fires on my unseen crack
Seems to warm from inside out to my back.
I want to shape my fingers in front of my jaw
And project bunny figures upon the wall.

Then he stopped his constant finger wave.
(Must have found a stalactite in the cave)
And removing his glovelett in his leisure
Announces "It's time for a small procedure".

"I'll set it up in one months time,
You'll see a surgeon friend of mine".
And this second opinion a finger slid
To find what the first one said was hid.

By now I was feeling cold and it may seem silly
That I was cooling off to their fingers, chilly.
I felt like a summer snack on their tables slick,
A human popsicle with a Dr.'s pointer for a stick.

I arrived at surgery and the nurse declared
"Go into that cubicle and strip down bare,
Pants tie in the front, the shirt ties in the rear."
She gave no advice for the robe and I thought that queer.

In a death row walk I went to pre-op
Into a rolling bed I was told to "hop."
Then a Kevorkian-like shadow stood by my bed.
(God, if you love me leave the sheet away from my head.)

He wheeled me down the hall (not very far),
To an electronic filled room they call the OR
Rolled me face down on a table like a whale's dead pup
And began strapping me down, so I couldn't get up.

"Do you have any allergies?" I told him just to red wine,
He laughed they were fresh out so I said, "a beer would do fine."
What I got was wires, tubes and hot towels that're so plump
It took my mind off the fact, they were shaving my rump.

All the gang was now gathered with gauze masks all in place
My mask was plastic and covered most of my face.
Then all the attention was fixed back at my posterior
As the bulldozer plowed from my ex to interior.

It was swiftly accomplished with just a few strokes,
With me the point of attention and the butt of their jokes.
They coiled up a bandage and stuffed it inside
With enough tape, once removed, that would strip off my hide.

That done, I was rolled away on my wheeled table
Coming to in the hallway (as best I was able)
The sign of "Recovery" was the most welcome I'd seen
Where I finally got my long awaited caffeine.

Now, how to leave like a hero after such a dissection?
(Ride a horse into the sunset was out of the question)
I pushed off the wheelchair in my John Wayneish talk.
I gathered up courage (and codeine) and out I did walk.

And now my recuperation is flourished in cards and in flower,
Though I can't sit to enjoy it, it's my shining hour.
With one concern on my mind, you dare ask what is it?
It's that hour-long, much-dreaded, postoperative visit.

The Start

You want to run?
What's wrong with you?
Does your mental machine need a tighter screw?

You run ten miles,
Where did you get?
You ended up where you began, but wet.

If you want to end
Where you began to start,
You can cut your time if you don't depart.

I see no need
For the rush and hustle
Cause I like my belly and my bustle.

I admire your stamina.
To you, I cheer.
But as you race by don't sweat in my beer.

A Doom no Man Should Face

My world is done, i sit alone
On a seat of cold stone stairs.
No use to pray as life slips away.
I watch it stain in the drain with my cares.

No need to leave or begin to bereave,
The somber clouds come and muffle the moon.
It was the worst of my fears and the cause of my tears,
Come and gone all too soon.

I hate breaking my last bottle of beer on a holiday weekend.

Learning at the Footstool

Put down the mouse pressed in your hand.
Let the laptop hit the floor.
To learn what's ahead look to your past,
And reopen an older door.

With humor new and wisdom aged,
It's not a superhighway but passive street.
You'll gain not from "C drive" what you could,
Sitting at your grandma's feet.

School teaches you some of what age knows of
And colors your life with hope (or dread)
The truer hue comes not from yellowed page
As it does from a grayer head.

Responsive wisdom from the ones once there
Offer answers to inquiring looks.
To fill the voids between the lines
Of assigned or assumed "great books."

The history lies waiting for you there
In a close and personal way.
So now, make the request, or you'll always regret
That you waited another day.

Of Lure and Lore

A man knows the cost of his fishing pole,
From the time he buys it till he's buried.
But finds it becomes much more valuable
The day after he gets married.

Pricetags on their Toes

I don't hesitate
To honestly state,
Folks planning funerals don't have too much fun.
But there was one man in the past
Who took time to ask
How much a nice funeral would run.

Not wanting to fight him
I broke it down item by item
Explaining how much each special service would cost.
Cutting out all the crap
On the way to a dirt nap
Caring carefully for the one he'd just lost.

I told him how " The Deluxe"
Would cost five hundred bucks
Inclusive of ten beautiful bouquets of flowers.
A selection of fourteen favorite hymns,
Plus tunes as the casket's rolled in
And a personal eulogy that goes on for hours.

Then there's one a bit blander
At two-sixty, I call " The Standard"
With two arrangements of flowers by my sister Lynn.
Two songs played to finish from start
That the organist now knows by heart,
And a textbook sermon with the dead's name sprinkled in.

The last is known as "The Thrifty"
Sets you back only fifty
I roll the casket through the church on it's journey to rest.
As the organist rehearses upstairs
The parson blurts out how God cares
And as the dead pass, slaps a marigold on his chest.

Angel Catchers

Sometimes my days are sleepy,
Other times the schedule's frantic.
But when you're in a steeple
Life is never so romantic.

If pigeon gifts get slippery,
Or when icing has begun
Let not these catchers get too fussy
And choose not to catch this one.

Even when my thoughts become unkind
And my language gets too rough.
I feel close to God in the spire alcoves.
And God, I feel for now that's close enough.

Lord, no matter what the "white throats" think of me,
Whether it's heathen, drunk or louse.
To slip and fall and crash through the roof,
Is no way to enter God's House.

Miss Thomas

She stands strong and proud in the center of town,
Conjoining time and space.
And although she's nearly ninety, now,
The only thing weathered is her face.

She's seen cold blizzards and warm hurricanes,
And rung in the New Years, one by one.
She watches each Memorial Day Parade
(Decoration Day, when she was young).

Aviators look for her on their return to town,
Likewise, sailors on the river.
Her song to them slows from time to time,
But those that love her do forgive her.

Her sparkle's there, her voice unchanged,
Her directing hands that don't slow down,
Keep beckoning friends and strangers, too,
This grand old dame in town.

Pantyhose Among the Departed

Should my remaining days be filled with gloom
I brighten remembering the cemetery as a dressing room.
I thought it was great though others figured it queer,
To be treated to peeks of a black brassiere.

She had a slim figure and a face soft as a rose
And showed no shame at all slipping into pantyhose.
Then sat cross-legged and smiling by the water pump
Showing all of her legs and most of her rump.

In a motion I'd take otherwise a flirt
She slithered right out of her mini skirt,
Followed close by her blouse and without turning around,
Pulled up and zipped up, in a long formal gown.

Strutting and smiling with gentle breeze in her hair
Never knowing or caring 'bout this man standing there.
And if reincarnation happens before my soul to heaven ascends,
My wish is to return as a camera lens.

Brenda

If ever an angel found a worldly birth,
It'd be this young fairy that landed on earth.
With a wee giggle that brightens the darkest of place
And a smile that infects the most somber of face.

A fierce lovely lass that appears to be shy,
But her peace, shared with others, tends to magnify.
She makes better my brother, to whom she is bound
And enriches the world just from being around.

Towards the end of an evening, she'll serve Irish Mist.
Each guest leaving the cottage all turn for a kiss,
Thankful for this heart filled with love, in the size of a toy,
Brought to our family, by marriage, is such a great Joy.

Summer Love

Buck moon filled the sky,
Fourth of July,
After fireworks and picnics it was just you and I.

Nights on the phone,
Just from feeling alone,
Talk of a dream house becoming a home.

Letters and rhymes,
Good and bad times.
Enough smiles and tears to change her name to mine.

But they're just memories that fade with dawn and fall like the dew,
Now I'm without you.
I'm out on my own
Not going home, anymore.

The President of the United States

I've come to Washington at this rather late hour,
Viewing senatorial chairs varnished by seats of power.
I'll miss the wisdom and wit from all the high places
So eloquently expressed from both sides of their faces.
From the senators gently bending over the pages
To the Christian-right heads, harder than rock of ages.

I prefer to meet with the President, so calm and so cool
As Secret Servicemen guard skinny-dipping in the reflecting pool.
Of his liberal coating of his dreams for this nation
And lack luster performance, I've had more than my ration.
He changes the Army but won't change his ways
(He changes his official stand at least ten times each day)
Why, he's taken six years just to hire a staff.
I could match wits with him and in fairness, only use half.

We'll leave him there two more years to avoid drafts and smoke pot
To cheat on his wife (Father of our country, he's not)
But there's a draft he can't dodge when January winds start to howl,
When on the Capitol steps, he meets President Powell.

and Senators

Where's Connecticut's senior Senator when the voting's begun?
Out drinking with Massachusetts' third favorite son?
When our nation first called him did he come forward to meet it?
Or did he run off to part-timers, and did he complete it?
He asked his father's guidance the time he came up 1A,
His dad said "why not run" but didn't mention which way.
So the man ran for office and knew political leap-toading
(I'd use the word "frog" but for him I feel swamps are foreboding)
He studied late into the night by the light of Ted's fridge,
And they were inseparable until the car left the bridge.
Over and over he wins every race that he has run,
Run to the store for more Grecian Formula 2001.
Holding parties for the party is the limit of his pervue.
Small wonder there's no time left to sit down and serve you.

Charlie

Charlie sat down on the wicker seat, and rocked
Slowly in his old chair.
If not for the creaking of the oak
You'd not guess that he was there,
As he is each night at ten to nine
A smile and tradition does he bring,
This master of the Meetinghouse
Held slave to curfew's ring.

The bell rope sways in the evening breeze
Through the massive open door.
His hands flex for duty on the line
His father pulled before.
Experience and girth are anchoring
To hold this Sexton on the floor.
Not like the lighter ringers now
Taking flight while at the chore.

Charlie's rung out the end of wartime,
For Presidents on the way to rest.
He's pealed them in for brides and grooms
And tolled for mourners' sad requests.
I now hold Mr. Adams' honored job
And I keep the steeple locked
To preserve, protect and in great respect
Keep well, his bell and clock.

Easter

The ministers had supper Friday night,
Though I didn't know earlier.
So the bread for the feast
Had to be shipped in by courier.

The package store had closed,
But with egos, divine,
They laid hands on the water
So's to turn it to wine.

The liquid would not ferment.
But they accept no defeat.
"Don't the women of Rome,
Crush the grapes with their feet?"

A larger vessel was called for
(Of course I had to do it)
And the group was quite shocked
When their feet went right through it.

"Let me try charming with music"
The minstrel said, but alas
The music 'twas so loud
That it shattered the glass.

So they formed a support group
For the spill on the floor.
Shoved the bread in their mouths
As they made for the door.

Then one asked "Who's to pay
For our time, money and loss?"
So they dragged me out back
And nailed me up on a cross.

And they heard me exclaim
As they walked out of sight,
"You may have screwed up your evening,
But you got *my* part right."

The Late-Night Shopping Trip

I went to do some shopping
At an all-night grocery store.
I had no awakened family
I had no coffee, no soda and more.
So I picked my carriage with square wheels
(my luck always follows suit)
I dumped in Folgers and some Pepsi
And headed to the aisle marked "fruit."

There a shortened skirt and lengthened leg
I happened upon by chance.
A tight sweater and long curls of blonde
Persuaded more than casual glance.
Her purse bounced proudly as she walked away,
Upon a bottom, round and ample
But when she turned, 'tween peach and plum
I saw an Adam's Apple.

I picked up my pace to leave this place
When her cherry lips broke to a smile.
(Now, I was never one to stay in shape
But I could have easily run ten miles.)
My items flew through the bar code scan
As I strove to escape the strange.
I threw a fifty for ten dollars worth
And told the clerk to keep the change.

Once in the safety of my truck
I downed a Pepsi in one swig,
Cheated from flirtatious thoughts
By the shopper in a wig.
If just viewed from behind I'd follow lane to lane,
And mentally unwrapped her,
Never knowing all along the way
This young "belle" possessed a clapper.

But my shock must pale in comparison
As to what his wife must think,
When in bed she's in her flannels
And turns to see him "in the pink."
Then I wonder, in the evening
When feeling amorous in their room,
Who pulls the lace across who's face
And who does what to whom.

I remove the parcels from my pickup
(and thoughts of prancing Goldilocks)
I slipped into bed and saw my wife
In my tee shirt and Army socks.
I too am guilty. I cut short my list.
I too have goods and bads.
But I'll explain to the wife why I could not pick up
Her feminine hygiene pads.

Fat Chance

I can remember a multitude of tasks
But can't recall a detail of things you never asked.
I can anticipate foul weather and when sunshine may resume.
I can second guess your late requests but can't read what you assume.

I hear you (when you are here) of problems with the rules.
But to support your carnivals, written requests are vital tools.
Written history and instructions have superseded campfires tribal,
To correct and protect, and in retrospect, is probably why they *wrote*
the Bible.

So I ask the same (in verse, quite lame) to this end let us work so well,
To keep this church a heaven on earth, and not my job a living hell.

The Cadet

On greystone by the river Hudson,
In the misty morning shroud
Stands a long gray line of men now.
Like the oaks they're strong and proud.

Through text and timber they've been tested.
In Lee's footprints they have trod,
Aware of commitment to conquer evil,
Overseas and under God.

Are they prepared? Oh, yes, they are sir.
Are they ready? Time will tell.
Each one now holds the key to Heaven,
Yet has the will to charge the gates of hell.

"Your mission is first, the troops come second."
Follow these words right to the letter.
But keep the heart of a lion and the soul of a woman,
And both concerns survive, together.

So take the misery of the rain and the baking sun,
And the long, dark gloom of night.
For if, this day, they're yours to treasure,
Then Lieutenant, you won the fight.

Glory

In reflections of our historical reasonings,
This melting pot holds the strangest seasonings.
Crime and violence, bigotry and cheating.
And on ourselves, the Liberty crown we laud,
That we're founded on freedom, under God.
As though the truth comes from the words, repeating.

Yes, First Sergeant

I was on the company street
One bright and sunny day,
Awaiting new troops I was flanked,
By Sergeants Russell and Deprey.
The busses came to a roaring stop
And disgorged green, young troops,
With fear etched in their faces
And new pants full of bags and droops.

Drill Sergeants fired orders
At kids that did not understand,
On how to lock up their heels in unison
Or what to do with their shaking hands.
My eyes stabbed right through them, forward
With a body rigid as carved stone.
On a raised platform there before them,
I stood there, all alone.

I felt their eyes glued to me
And when they stood fast in place,
I barked "Life as you know it is over
And shut that big hole in your face."
Each new soldier must be oriented.
Each new pair of pants earn a stool.
I've only eight weeks to mold them
Into killers, cold and cruel.

I spoke out clear and loud what I wanted.
Discipline, their minds, their soul.
I'd teach them to eat crap and like it
How to live and not die in a hole.
I'd be both their mother and father
I'd be their instructor and their priest.
I'd guide them to "three S" in five minutes
And how time off, here and now, will cease.

Then a move in the ranks was detected,
As a new troop bolted out from the crowd.
I came about and stared at Sergeant Russell
Indicating clear and loud,
"Your weapon" and Russ tossed his rifle,
I caught it while turning around.
I hollered "Halt" while sighting the barrel
Then with one shot brought the new soldier down.

I cleared the weapon and handed it back then
Turned to the crowd that couldn't believe.
I stared straight ahead, without blinking
And ordered Russell and Deprey to "Retrieve"
The two non-comms broke out in a dead run
As game as a prize racing horse.
Silent eyes followed the green, flowing figures
As they roughly dragged away the fresh corpse.

"Let that be the last of our problems"
As I brought order back into its place.
"Your platoon sergeants will get you to quarters,
And shut that big hole in your face."
Executing a perfect about face
I went to my office and slowly stepped in,
Put my feet on my desk and drank coffee,
Then I allowed myself a grin.
I loved doing that to new soldiers
To get their attention on the first day.
Getting their hearts and minds to follow
Is easier when you do it that way.

But I owe a case of cold beer and a jug to
The soldier that ended up dead.
It's always another battalion's Drill Sergeant
In baggy fatigues and damn near shaved head,
That I convince to play a fresh newbie
And with duffel, into ranks was slipped.
Was given orders to fall when the blank "hit" him
And all the rest of the script.

So now each of these troops will take orders
Every one that is written or said.
To win at getting their feet firmly planted,
Sometimes you first have to play with their head.

Home

Bunks three high, shoulder width apart
Gear and men dropped in at night.
Not enough room to breathe much less move,
And damned so little light.

The water smells like chlorine bleach
(Two gags and then you swallow)
A wide-eyed nightmare walks you through the dark
To carry you to tomorrow.

Concrete pipes rammed down into the ground
Laced with limestone once a week
Covered with screen and filled with stones.
Still for miles around it wreaks.

Bored and scared and lonesome and tired
You color in one day,
On the calendar charting your return
To a home so far away.

Night doesn't fall, it grows out of the grass
And surrounds the lifeless trees
Deafening senses and keeping you safe,
Then lifts on the back of the morning breeze.

Survive the torturing learning hours
Of the three hundred sixty-five days
And find, in the world, with your family near
That "home" is thousands of miles away.

Living and Dying in a Hole

Few words describe the horror of seeing friends you cannot save,
Second only to the thoughts one has when digging their own grave.
Exhilarating desperation in burrowing for all you're worth
Till it's armpit high, halfway to hell, in the chaos and the earth.

In silence of that solitude there is no marching fife and drum,
Not looking out you look within for the animal you've become.
Bastard badgers in a dirt cocoon fighting other bastard's fights.
Not with tearing teeth or scalpel claws but with eyes down barrel
sights.

The pounding of the thundering rain shakes the hole, and too,
the man.
Birds of war shriek in the night igniting everyone they can.
The fields of fire go back to black, can't see the hand before your face,
But you can't allow yourself to rest lest it be your final resting place.

The crickets stop, your heart beats loud, your breath now comes in
spurts.
You strain to hear for someone near or the bugs' resuming chirps.
Bushes come to life and shadows move in your intent and squinting
eyes.
Will detail show an unnoticed tree or a muzzle flash surprise?

Alone together with thirty-five, all strangers without smiles,
Lack of speech between the FPLs make meters into miles.
Scratching eyelids and gunmetal mouth (the canteens content tastes
like puke)
I should be in "the world" and in my bed. Why doesn't Congress
drop a nuke?

This hole is home forever and I never want to leave.
If I can't climb out at daybreak who the hell would care to grieve?
Home is where the heart is and my pump is in this crater,
I'm the power and the glory of all I survey and don't care what might come later.

First light grows slowly in the east but the wee one's whistle starts to blow.
The charge brings changes to third eyes so's not to miss the show.
The air around itself explodes in a shower of evil wrath,
The crack of too close yet not close enough passes in a meteor path.

The thud and ripping knocks you back into a sea of goo,
To remind, that excavation hours ago was dug for holding two.
Don't let your brain go wandering in the lighter prior days
Or you'll join in his relaxation and his peaceful, silent gaze.

Now young man draw out your bayonet and make another's mother sick.
Hell's holiday cut the distance as your hammer fell to just a click.
Take one more smiling hero on your road to be the best.
Your CIC will view you during supper with gushing glory on your chest.

For years of cemetery celebrations your name's now on the role,
They'll speak of duty, honor, country and how you gallantly left your hole.
You went proud and tall and standing, not to surrender, yield or grovel.
When all you wanted was a hole back home, and not to have to use *your* shovel.

The New Army

Who's to say that we cannot change?
We've got earrings on soldiers and computers on the range.
Patent leather shoes with our green business suits.
And you're out if you even raise your voice at recruits.
"Don't wear the cap with your blues cause you might just loose it."
Leave the colors out at night, it's okay to abuse it.

Politics and soldiering have never agreed.
One's meant for slow moves the other for speed.
Salesmanship and leadership don't coincide.
Arm-twisting pitches never resulted in pride.

NCOs had a good record on guarding this nation
Back when experience in your background outweighed education,
To determine the leaders in war and in peace.
But now it's assumed that your college-age niece,
Can come to the fore and turn tides in battle,
'Cause she's user friendly and IBM compatible.

I joined this corps in its near darkest day.
Racial riots, lack of discipline and morale in decay.
Since, I've seen many great strides in correcting these wrongs,
Putting power back down in the hands it belongs.
Sergeants' Business fought that battle and must do again,
Power down or your regiments will rust in the rain.

Lead by example not by exception.
Ask your soldiers to fight, not hold a reception.
All of your old bulls stand ready and strong.
Too much of the new stock has been coddled too long.
Challenges, not comfort, bring soldiers to arms,
We must fire them up to respond to alarms.

We decide the direction that we go with this corps.
Leave your civilian ideas on the hook by the door.
Human elements not electronics turned the tide in each war,
And will do so again, just as before.
Perseverance and pride are our by words, not lore.
So give it honor, give completely, then give it some more.

Together

One said:

If we all worked together no one would ever wait.
And if we all worked together we'd be nothing short of great.
If we all worked together it would set a positive tone.
And if we all worked together this place would seem like home.

And I replied:

If we all worked together it couldn't get much worse
And if we all worked together I wouldn't have to curse.
But if we all worked together, in fear, I would call a nurse
'Cause if we all worked together it would certainly be a first.

Pimps

In January I'll make a New Years resolution,
To no longer condone my wife's dog prostitution.
The poor puppy has barely reached a full four years old,
And before she is bred the wife's got all the pups sold.

Isn't it right that I fight for no strange dog to molest her
While pimps on the side grin with pride at the kennel club register?
Secrets hid like they did in the south long before,
Well God bless me, learn from history, those folks lost the war.

I'm not convinced that, in a Panama hat driving the bitch in for her
seeding,
That this bastard (what else) is not from the same stock himself and
continuing just more inbreeding.

Connecticut, my Connecticut

Will a "Connecticut Food" now save the state,
Beyond the Governor's would or coulding?
Considering economic straws he's grabbed to date,
I think we should adopt "Indian Pudding."
"Lobster" is used and so's foul "Boston Beans"
Did they improve Maine or Mass? How do we know?
Will our elected rear ends improve our means
By naming a state food "Clams Casino"?

Will popping Indian corn or boiling buffalo tongues
Keep our economic ills under wraps?
And have a Thanksgiving Day feast like when the country'd begun
Realizing the tables are all used for "craps"?
We'd be better off offering more substance than flash,
And keep present employers from rambling.
To count on more solid futures instead of quick cash
And draw Connecticut businesses, other than gambling.

Ding Dong

You got jelly in the peanut butter
You spilled beer down on my pup
You got water marks on Grandma's table
You left the toilet seat up.

You're late from work and dinner got cold
So late you can't take your check for deposit
The car ran out of gas 'cause you didn't fill up
And the clothes pole fell down in the closet.

The faucet's still dripping down in the sink
The dryer's still on the fritz
The bulb is still out in the hallway upstairs
Is there anything you've got time to fix?

Wife, the house was on fire, so I put the seat down
(close to the water because it's made out of lumber)
I took the battery out of the smoke alarm
Just so's not to disturb your slumber
I latched all the windows and turned out the lights
And as my final chore
As I tiptoed out to get in the truck
I double locked the front door.

Haunted

Billy Beadle lived long ago,
But did not let his clan do so.
He took his ax and chopped them one by one
Then swallowed the barrel of his gun.

Though Wethersfield has seen strange sights,
None transcend the stormy nights
In the boneyard his ax catches the lightning's glow,
As Billy seeks to send the next below.

Little Big Man

He had the heart of a giant
And a lion's voice
A smile as big as the country
He came to by choice.
Strength in values were his
His arms were even stronger
And after years telling stories of soccer
They got even longer.
He used to bet money
And collect only a laugh
As he'd grip phone books (by the bindings)
And rip them in half.
We used to go fishing
When he was still here
And devote the summer evening
To dine on flounder and beer.
At his cottage table
With him, the night I'd spend
Never so close to a man
Who was so close to his end.

The night that he died
He shoveled snow from the barn door
(Would it have lessened the outcome
If I came an hour before?)
It was a two-sided pain
That I felt with his loss
You see, he was more than a friend
He was also my boss.
Tearfully I began to plow snow
Then I heard thunder rumbling
"Damn, chief .. you only been there an hour
And already God's grumbling."

Unmutual Funds

I've got a dollar in my pocket!
Been there so long I almost forgot it.
All rolled up in a neat little ball,
Surprised I found it there at all.

I unrolled it, flattened it and you might have guessed it,
I put it on the ironing board and pressed it.
If she knew I had it she'd flare and scold,
So I'll slip it into my billfold.

When she has money she's spending, you can't stall it.
This note should be safe there in my wallet.
It's worn and scribbled on and looks quite homely
And in my care it'll always be lonely.

Wish I could find another buck
For this one to mate
But the way my luck runs,
It'd just masturbate.

The Trestle and Me

Just another Saturday with the Cub Scout dressed up band
We followed our leader by the river with fishing gear in hand
Rocks did roll, the dust did fly as through the prickers we did wrestle
To get our angling done and badges won, we had to cross ... a trestle.

With questions behind, my widened eyes in fear I could not hide
I proposed we climb down and cast out far and let the fish swim
from the other side.
I guess our leader could not hear through hairy ears both filled
with wax
As he issued clear instructions on how we could walk the tracks.
He spoke of measured steps, not looking down and keeping one ear
open,
As the first three members of the band began their slow and shaky
gropin'.

Now I had never fished before nor walked railroad tracks like tramps
Mom just bought my tackle the other day with ten books of her
Green Stamps.
I thought I might just sit this out and come back another day,
But my leader called from halfway across to start to make my way.

Eight were across, just Gess and me left behind, wearing a long and
sheepish mask,
My feet started out with no desire to be next, but I'd be damned if
I'd be last.
Foot by foot I inched myself seeing water rushing below my feet.
I felt like puking but the ties were slippery enough without giving
them that treat.

It was about the bridge's middle I heard the leader scream with scorn,
And above that din, almost from within, I thought I heard ... a horn.
The leader waved me on with new found zeal while looking in the other direction,
Mentioning I'd better hurry in a voice quite clear but with soprano-like inflection.

I looked back and saw Gess climbing down to the safety of where we started
Our leader continued to shout, a closer horn drowned him out, and then I more than farted
Feeling this just won't do I took the rail ties by two figuring time's running out, by heck,
Looking at the tracks at both ends, where then soon went to bends, is when I fell to the unholy deck.

My tackle box took sail, my pole crashed 'tween the rails and I landed square on my nose
As I prayed for delivering, noticed the tracks were now quivering, sprayed ammonia and up I arose.
I still did not know which track, from the front or the back, or how deep was the water for diving
So I squatted between two sets of tracks and waited it out as my best bet for ever survivin'.
The giant roared round the curve with me pushing reverse, happy with my final selection
But my smile faded soon and took cheer to deep gloom when I heard a horn in the other direction.
The first train passed me by as my bobber did fly between the wheels as if it were floating
And in the relative clear I got up off my rear to see in the water, my gear box was now boating.

I got down on the far bank as the next choo choo tank came churning along in its glory,
Gess got over with the rest, said my trip was the best, but there's just a bit more to the story.
They got to cast and catch fish as our original wish, from the sandy shore or the big rocks
I threw out with no luck (rookies casts sure do suck) trying to catch my Green Stamp tackle box.

My Cooking

Some tell me in their homes they blow out the screens
After picnicking on my homemade baked beans
I feed them plates of brown stick to ribs style goo
They laugh, "Tastes more like the stuff that gets stuck to my shoe."

So now I'll not offer a "Hi there, how are ya,"
And not offer you over for my Jambalaya.
No skin off my nose, I feel no great loss,
If you prefer not to partake of my barbecue sauce.

Where you acquired your taste bud, God only knows.
You'd think I buttered the rolls with the jam 'tween my toes.
Give your attitude to others because I'll just not take it.
I'll slap more roadkill to the gas grill because I just love it.

I'll stink my yard up like fish, blue, gold, flat or sworded
If you think your next invitation's pre-posthumously awarded.
And if you die of the food that from my house you had,
I'll throw your haunch on the fire to see if you, too, taste bad.

Lori

There's a time in every father's life
When his son leaves home to take a wife.
> When she takes half his name and all his time.
Will she be good enough in giving joy
To this man you've raised from a bawling boy?
> Seems tantamount to a federal crime.

But you look beyond your selfish pain
And recognize just what you've gained
> Thinking of neither as a child.
They've got future plans, so well thought through
And a strong commitment they've held to
> And all the time ... she makes him smile.

No one at this ceremony could feel cheated
As in the church you're closely seated
> Listening to phrases tried and true.
As on life's road they've just begun
I really have not lost a son,
> I found a daughter, new.

Graduation

Pomp and Circumstance, caps and gowns.
In the entire crowd there are no frowns.
Now young man, take a graduated breath
You now know the difference between C and F.

Boats

It's hard to bluefish for a man like me,
My feet were made for the land not for the sea.
My brothers think me quite a bore
To keep them landlocked here on shore.

I like my fishing without frills
So I breathe through my mouth, not by way of gills.
My feet and seat and rod on rock,
Make me pleased and alive and dry of sock.

From all that I have ever wrote
You'll never hear of my love of a boat.
I'm happy and restful with thanks everlasting
For the Joe long ago that thought up, surfcasting.

Tom tells me that even God's only Son,
To speak to a crowd pushed off in one.
Hey, Tom! they poked holes in Him and Communion bled.
And I say, only folks with holes in their head,
Would leave the safety of the ground,
To catch a fish you can buy for a buck a pound.

On the East coast the earth doesn't rock or roam,
And when bait and beer are out, you just walk home.
I'm not going shipping for cod or tuna,
Or increase my chance to see Jesus sooner.

Baptism

You cried continuously and kicked, and yet
The clergy smiled and tickled you and got you wet.
You should be proud one so young took a firm stand
And anointed the ministers other hand.

Bridges

When I was young and Mom drove us far,
I'd cross the bridges from the floor of the car.
The reason for this I can't explain.
But to this day the urge remains.

Did I think the construction was incomplete?
Or that the automaker should install floatation seats?
I'd rather walk a lightning storm on a stormy ridge,
Than ride in a car across a bridge.

I hear death bells and their peals
When I take empty high roads on four wheels.
My preference'd be to fly in a plane, unsound,
Than to auger my Ford into the ground.

If you thought of this, I guess you'd know
I can't see the drop from the floor below.
Or maybe the reason, after all
Is, when beneath the seat, it's a shorter fall.

Sympathy

I join you in your grief today
And sent a card to simply say.
Loving thoughts of you whirl in my head,
But I'm really glad your husband's dead.

Good Bye

Damp eyes for a life so soon to close,
Are known and understood.
But a tortured heart's too much to bear
Even when the choice you made was good.

Defenseless, sitting all alone
On the side of a strange, new bed.
Scant in luggage coming in
Knowing well, they're leaving dead.

The disinfectant atmosphere
We all work up to, now or later.
It takes a twist of truth, or a twisted mind
To twist their arm to sign the paper.

I wrench my hands in wretched ways,
And attempt a conversation,
As she selects a bed for sleep, and death,
Through eyes of resignation.

I love her still but leave her now
As a burst emotion burns my eye.
The truth was clear in her quiet voice,
"Good as any place to die."

Young Once

An ice cream cone melting on the sidewalk's heat.
A mom slapping a son, trying hard not to cough.
A father hitting his baby for crying in a passing car.
I want to stop them, then break their arms off.

If they have no patience for rearing a child,
(and patently make rear ends of themselves)
Why not get yourself neutered like alley cats and dogs
And put their reproductive glands on the shelves.

Nothing brings up emotions from down within
Or drives my heart to break
As 'grown-ups" beating, scarring or ignoring their own.
It's like a child's cry on a dark, frozen lake.

Instead of chilling your children and making them cold
Why not freeze your sperm and eggs?
For if she saw into the future to see how you "love,"
She wouldn't have let you between her legs.

Firsts

A purple bud within a breast of snow
A neighborhood's attention to coming glory.
Aspirations for the cold to go
And warm dreams of summer's story.
The mediocre bloom of crocus cup
(of all flowers, no better or worse)
We're jubilant with it's coming up
For just in it's being first.

The lovers of firsts brush back the white
That for months has blown around,
Forgetting November's annual right,
Of heralding the first flakes falling down.
We need to stop and love each display,
As we would be poor fishermen,
To prolong admiration for the first catch on opening day,
So's to never fish again.

Brides Letter from the Best Man

Years ago we separated
And just before I flew
He and I, in desperation
Tore a dollar bill in two
For one to signal the other
To "rush and cover my tail"
Should he receive the other half
By messenger or mail.

I'm confident you'll never need it
Or the awesome strength and power
For help or communication
With him at any hour
And when the date comes on the next year
Pull this out and have a laugh
Think how much brighter both your lives are
Then when I was his "other half."

Long Ago

The early winter filled our home,
With classic New England weather.
We had a lot more love than money on,
The first Christmas we shared together.
We bought a pine tree at the firehouse,
And she named it Charlie Brown,
We picked out a small box of ornaments,
From the hardware store in town.
Her mom gave us lights to string on it,
And I plugged them in behind the chair,
And after putting the silver balls on every third limb,
It still looked awfully bare.

The next morning came the same disappointment,
So we drove north in our old car.
We still had more love than money,
So we couldn't drive too far.
We spoke now and again of our small, sad tree,
And how it looked so stark.
Not having enough to do anything else,
We pulled into a wooded park.
Getting out in the cold, her hand I did hold,
And we took a long, wintry walk.
Crunching down on the pine needles as we stepped,
She suddenly broke off our talk.

She lifted a pinecone in her hand
And smiling, she said to me,
"With some paint and glitter and a little love,
We could hang these on our tree."
I thought it was dumb but I helped her collect
Some of these dry woodland treasures.
We picked up about twenty and I actually had fun
Sharing in her simplest of pleasures.
She didn't stop grinning after we got in the car
As a light snowfall did begin.
She kissed my cheek, and I held her close
(And the one that she held, within).

The trailer that night filled with pinecones and glue,
Cocoa, cookies and a small glass of wine.
With yarn tied to their tops we hung them all up.
To us, that small tree did look fine.
We no longer looked down on the tiny tree,
It was the best we'd ever seen.
Just a walk in the woods in the cold, and in love
Made it special and glimmer and gleam.

The ornaments still survive today,
And they're the ones we hold dear and savor.
We still have more love than money, as then
And may it never swing to the "bucks" favor.

Audrey

Audrey at thirteen had a friend, her imagination would send
For visits to the meadow not far away
"Together" they would move along to where the grass grew cool
and long
And till early in the evening they would stay.
Summer nights up on the hill
Audrey Goodwell lying still
Complete with a friend all her own.

When Audrey turned sixteen, with a boyfriend she'd be seen
Strolling hand and hand 'round the setting sun
On the town green in shadows long he would sing a loving song
And walked her to the meadow when nighttime had begun
Summer nights up on the hill
Audrey Goodwell lying still
Complete with a friend all her own.

When winter winds were blowing' Audrey left her house, alone
At least there's just one set of tracks out in the snow
With no one there to hold, she laid down in the meadow's cold,
Dreamt of summer's warmth and let her troubles go.
Summer nights up on the hill
Audrey Goodwell lying still
Complete with a friend all her own.

Class of 1970

The spirit of 1970 is still vibrant and alive
But experienced in love and life at 1970 plus twenty-five.
We've traveled miles since cap and gown and the day we stood so
proud
Knowing so much more than the gray, fat folks that sat out in the
crowd.

Some of us went north, others went to school, still others joined the
service,
Some took a job or wandered far because our parents didn't deserve us.
We searched for love and found divorce and now split time with
our kiddies.
Our parents still don't understand, how could they, they're old
biddies.

Now, as naked in the bathroom mirror it can be clearly seen
We may be forty-three years old, but to us, we still look eighteen.
We still sport dark hair and it does not thin, at least we think it's so
Or could it be our folks were right and your eyes are the first to go?

We attended commencements this past June and saw our own kids
cross the stage
And wonder in their excited state if they now judge our age.
Did they see thick waistlines, advanced foreheads and a wrinkle
here or there?
I think they did and spoke of it not because they know they'll soon
be here.

The Pain Inside the Closet

There's a home I used to visit
To withdraw love but not deposit.
Though laughter echoed in the halls
There was a pain inside the closet.

The group inside were separate and strong
But in no time grew very small.
Their holidays drew dark with flowers
Till there was little left at all.

The closets emptied and empty heart,
That began to search and stray.
We grew apart in time and life
Though never far away.

The pain inside the closet now
Has come through better for the fire.
Dissatisfied with treading troubled seas,
She climbed out just one step higher.

She retains my love and has gained respect
For becoming stronger, but not tough
And for sharing with me her challenged smile
That is more than fair enough.

Reflections

The autumn leaves are involved in their annual show,
From the maple trees out back.
Their reflection in the window, though
Is dismal in shades of gray and black

It's like bombings, from the air they're beautiful
Like God's fireworks all around.
But they seem a great deal less spiritual
When seen from on the ground.

It's a small man with lower worth and vision
Living eight hours a day then flees it.
Worrying not about his own task or decision
But how another person sees it.

When each does their best at their small part
Well or not, the world turns 'round.
Improve through practice your chosen art
Don't worry if someone else thinks it's sound.

Prior Planning Prevents Piss-Poor Performance

Knock before entering
Think before asking
Cause I'm not your agent
For last minute tasking

If you're credited and praised
For the ship you are sailing
Check your log and your compass
Before whipping me for your failing

So, you people of letters
Please remember these
Your life will be better
If you know the SIX P's

Smiling Sam

He's a balding old man, a stagnant old codger,
(He puts off comments like bald. His foreheads getting larger).
If we're to tighten our belts why is he gaining weight?
Can it be, just to hear him we spend two hundred a plate?

He's got a grand home and a driver. Who says crime never pays?
As he increases our taxes to vote himself a raise.
Is our memory so short we forget bad judgement and sin?
That we overlook years of robbery and let the thief in?

Don't tell me I'm wrong, it happens before our eyes,
He sells our soul to the devil and terms it compromise.
"That's how we do business in this grand, hallowed place"
Wiping egg and confusion off of his face, and his face.

Why not murder with a ballot? Why not kill with your vote?
Take these royals to the ramparts and drop them in the moat.
It's political insurrection readied for deployment.
They talk of feeling our pain, let them feel unemployment.

What do you think of his planning? I think there's been none from
his heart.
What about his execution? Now hey, there's a start.
This system in D.a C.apitol wouldn't seem deceiving or crass,
If while making their speeches they held guns and wore masks.

... and Her

The vampire has landed and she's making a speech
On not sucking our blood as she's gritting her teeth
She's from a great state based on trade, Indians and whaling
And she'd be a ship's Captain if she wasn't so accustomed to bailing.
She's "killing herself" every Washington day,
And to her constituents, I implore, don't stand in her way

Commentary on Confusion

The grand stage for election is set,
With the self-appointed upon it.
And we babe-in-the-woods balloteers,
Can only sort through the same vomit.
Pompous men say they'll now energize,
(Values and ethics, belated)
With their positions and promises
All regurgitated.

You speak on and bore us
For what seems to be hours
On the problems facing this nation
And the "these," "thems" and "ours."
Let us take back the reigns
From these smiling drop-pantsers.
You see, sirs, we *live* the issues,
We just want some *answers.*

All that they plan to do,
And what you've tried to do fires from your throat
While your ambition and drive ends
On the day you take the oath.
I'd cheer if just one of you
Whether veteran or novice
Could address your comments to accomplishments
Through the day that you leave office.

Shall politicians grant enlightenment
And for our innocence grieve?
As we, just everyday citizens
Are simply labeled naive.
Or can we right the country
More like Jefferson wrote
By selecting a leader
With them earning our vote.

My ballot is sacred
And for you it is reserved
Not with winning election
But more in how you will serve.
The future continues to be bright
(fueled on fossil body spoils)
And old career politicians
Could better serve us as oil.

School

You may find instant gratification
In purchase of home, car, suit or dress.
But don't push or shove, cajole or lie
In your aspirations of a child's success.

Educators in their well-trained line
Of optimums and level ones
Purloin the joys of the journey of life
In prodded races filled with dead runs.

To reproduce great intellectuals
To overachieve in every grade
Can you be proud, there at the end
With the product you have made?

We're losing components of quality
Pushing for straight A's across the land
Concentrating on the coveted mind
And disregarding heart and hand.

The Common Cup

I was in my office at work on my filing
When a new soldier barged in the door,
"First Sergeant, Dudley just hung himself
He's in on the shower floor."
I double-timed down the hallway
as if this is something brand new
You usually get an attempt in each class
But this was the fifth and it's still just week two.

I entered the latrine and shower
Smooth as a summer's breeze
But became enraged to see this sight
Of a faker down on his knees.
Looking up at me, coughing
Not ready to turn deep blue or bloat
His belt tied to the shower *handle*
And the other end looped round his throat.

"He's not dead, he's not even close yet
But he's a sick one, I do guarantee."
I untied the belt from the shower
"Okay Rover, come on, follow me."
Down the corridor to my office
I walked my new found dog.
He started crying instead of coughing
As I reached for CQ's report log.

I slammed the door behind us
(As if that were some new deal)
Brought the pup to the chair in front of my desk
And commanded for him to "Heel".
I calmly sat down and faced him
With his leash still around his neck,
I took a sip of my coffee and asked
"Aren't you happy here troop, what the heck?"

"I can't take it anymore, First Sergeant,
All this hollering, day and night."
I bellowed "If that's your way to get out, you're a no-go
So now, let's get it done right."
"In this desk there's a drawer full of goodies
For your type of desperation.
I got a straight razor, some rope and a hammer
Tools for about any occasion."

"Now, I don't recommend the hammer
If you don't hit your head square - well, you look dumb,
The rope takes some tricky knot tying
And you proved you can't do it, on your first run.
So that leaves us with just the razor,
You can practice with something duller, of course
You cut the long way, not across the wrist width
Or again, you'll look like the butt of a horse."

Dudley was just sitting there, silent
His jaw was way down to his chest.
"I'll go back and won't try it again, sir
And I'll really start doing my best."

"SIR?!?, who are you talking to dummy
You've got to see these six stripes, and you call
Me a sir - I ought to kill you myself now."
And I launched my coffee cup at the wall.

Before the shattered ceramic had settled
I took a long breath and started to shake,
I burned a hole in his head with my cold eyes
"Now just look at what you made me break."
I wailed "My grandmother gave that cup to me,
When I signed up to fight in the war,
Now the only gift I still had from my grandma
Is in pieces on my office floor."

"I'll give you this one chance to live, soldier,
Get out before the M.P.s come in."
"I'll pay for the cup, First Sergeant" he cried.
I yelled "I never want to see you again."
My clerk entered as Dudley ran for cover,
She cleaned the spill and the glass from the floor
I composed myself long enough to start smiling
And grabbed for a matching cup from my desk drawer.

Punishment push-ups motioning outside my window
Cadence shouted from marching troops on the malls
An insane commander blaring out on his trumpet
All sorts of long, loud Bugle Calls
Smells of summer and supper and Kiwi
And fresh Joe in my cup, all did blend.
How wonderful life is in the Army
How could anyone want all this to end?

940930

Wishes

I hope it rains like hell at my funeral,
Like it hadn't come down in years.
I'd be the only one dry and what's more I
Could pretend their wet cheeks were from tears.
And you see, the old folks, they have an expression,
'bout how Heaven opens up when it pours
So my chances are better at getting passed Peter,
If for another reason, he opens the doors.

Truth

There's a lot to be said for not saying much.

Black Potatoes

Was there ever a prouder race?
A stronger arm,
A fairer face,
Than the ones that we have seen,
Migrant heritage from the island, green.

Backs forged like steel from fighting wars,
Here in America,
Learned on their shores.
Ones the black potatoes could not kill,
Nor from frozen white upon green hills.

They built our canals and dug our mines,
Linked our coasts,
With railroad lines.
They wove sad tales of their bygones,
They fought and drank and sang sad songs.

They, that survived sick ships at sea,
Come here in rags,
Yet not on knees.
Passage out, as life, a token,
With families and their spirits broken.

The great Hunger forced them across the sea,
Not the dream
Of opportunity.
And if the crop would whiten from shades of black,
They'd pack their bags and travel back.

The Ballad of the Old Town Café

If you happen to drive south of Boston,
If north of New York you happen to stray,
If you find yourself needing a cold one,
Then just stop at the Old Town Café.

Don't let first impressions fool you,
By the darkness, décor or the air.
And, for God's sake, at noon, hold the bar top,
Lest the fire horn blow you out of the chair.

Cold bottles of beer are aplenty,
Draughts come complete with caps of foam.
Ball caps cover most of the patrons,
A place Archie Bunker would feel right at home.

The owner, looking much like a walrus,
Watches the flow of things, pint and quart,
Sitting at the back end with his cronies,
Holding sporting and political court.

A daily visitor sits by himself, there,
(the regulars just call him "the Grouch")
Paying his in nickels, dimes and quarters,
That he keeps tucked away in a pouch.

The know-it-alls of the whole sports world,
Gather 'round the one working door entrance,
Reeling off Red Sox and Yankee statistics,
And who in October's got the best chance.

The manager does his well-lit bookkeeping,
A big man, still playing sports,
In winter he plays "pneumonia-come-catch-me",
Walking in wearing just tee shirt and shorts.

The Breakfast Club is no longer in session,
Nor more Bucky, Boo Boo or the like.
To hear of the fires long past or war stories,
One must take the Heavenly Pike.

Retirees come in for the discount,
Roofers come in for the beer.
Former residents come in on occasion,
And are amazed the place is still here.

"No Harleys or other bikes on the sidewalk".
"If you gotta squirt, use the john not the trees".
"No harassing our beautiful bar maids".
The bar stool with the plaque's just for me.

So come in for the swift, friendly service.
Drop by for a shot and a beer.
Just remember the price of admission,
"What you hear, see or learn STAYS RIGHT HERE"!

Betsy Leaving

Was she, in fact dying,
Or was she living to the end?
Were her last words a pleasant greeting,
Or one last message, yet to send?

A body sick and tortured,
A wordless mouth so opened wide,
Bags of fluids at top and bottom,
Connected to tubes running down one side.

The family gathered 'round her,
Weeping tears she just cannot,
The quiet there between them tells
Unspoken vows 'ere to be forgot.

Then in the sullen stillness,
She valiantly raised her head
Her soft eyes gently opened,
Said "I love you", then fell dead.

The room filled with sobs and wonder
As they stared at her eyes, so blue
No question of the words she'd spoken,
But to whom she spoke them to.

Some assured she looked straight at them.
Others thought sure, it was to the world.
A few felt it was to her family, in whole,
But I truly knew this girl.

Her good-byes were stated days ago.
This final battle was hers, alone.
Her wonder and words were addressed to Him,
Then He walked her, gently home.

A Corpse in Brown Plaid

Last night while lying in my bed
I was visited by the dead.
He came not to haunt me, but to warn:
"You are not guaranteed the morn'."

I lay, not fearing, but alarmed
The figure was not threatening nor was he armed
His battledress faded and badly worn ... repeated:
"You are not guaranteed the morn'."

I was short of breath, long on convulse
I could feel the pounding of my pulse
Then, my nightmare done, I offed to sleep
Until it fell upon me deep

From time to time throughout the night
I dreamt about the ghastly sight
Echoing in my dreams, so torn,
"You are not guaranteed the morn'."

I woke before the sun's glorious pall
To a beautiful woman's soft, sweet call
Prior to the daylight, my ears did reap:
"This day may not be yours to keep."

Coming to an End

Swimming in a sea of bitterness
To the point I'd like to sue,
The fool from Heavens Wilderness,
The guardian angel assigned to you.

Each day, an anniversary
The first one without you there.
Strange thought of separation
As we were not an actual pair.

Hal's Angels 2000

To hear the chatter of our reunion
Hard to believe thirty years have passed.
The experiences, times and challenges
Since we were all together last.

Reliving through photos, slides and video,
All our happy, carefree days,
Before the photos were so yellow,
And our heads wore hues of grays.

The 360 months gone by now,
Many have been seeking love and wealth,
Some returned in strained relations
And not so perfect health.

But as each person shared their hardships
During this weekend of "coming home",
They expressed how their faith was strengthened
By knowing they were not alone.

So we face the road before us
And can still grow, as we grow older,
Knowing the voice that whispers to us
Is a Hal's Angel on our shoulder.

Snowflake

While wandering on a hillside,
I got a burr down in my sock.
To dispel the unholy hitchhiker,
I sat down on a rock,
I pulled up my cuff and off my shoe,
And left the pricker on it's own.
Then I saw a lovely flower,
Rooted in a crack of stone.

I called the bloom just "snowflake"
As I'd never seen its like,
In a garden, field or pasture,
While out fishing or on a hike.
Was it a miracle or revelation?
No, just a wonder, to me so rare,
At this unexpected garden,
Seeded itself here in my chair.

How could it get it's water
In a place we think so wrong?
Not to bake out in all the stone's heat,
And allow it to grow so strong.
I think God saved it from it's withering,
And guided away my hard, old boot.
He gives it love and understanding,
And gives this frail flower its root.

So let the precious petals, too,
Enjoy the marvel I hold so dear,
Not that she could be created,
But that she is with us here.
We may be reserved, too much, to say aloud,
The story she silently sings,
But don't let us hurry past snowflake,
Without knowing the beauty that she brings.

Liam

You are my younger brother,
Mom and Daddy tell me so.
Before you get much older,
There're a few things you should know.

I'm the one to educate you,
Cause I'm the one that's smart,
On how to drive Dad crazy with noises
And make him wonder "Was that a poop or fart?"

I'll teach you hiding mashed peas in diapers,
Making Mom think your dinner's done,
And how to howl just like a banshee,
When your little hand gets stung.

You need to know how to play with Riley,
When they think you are fast asleep.
You have to warm their hearts with smiling,
Before you even get your teeth.

Brothers need to share the secrets,
Of the best Christmas presents to get,
And how to pee upon a tree,
And not get your new sneaks wet.

I know they'll find wet spots in the bedding,
Warm spots in the pool, but honestly,
I want you to grow up in a hurry,
And be a boy as good as me.

A Song for Betsy

When life's travel comes more slowly, and
Of our experiences we take stock,
We find our most joyous journeys
Were merely hand in hand around the block.

We are forever in fluid motion,
Making many houses home.
Friendships and careers seem to come and go
As down our path we roam.

Photographs and minds memory
Bring back evergreens of passed Decembers.
Sight and thought are fleeting things,
It's the heart that always remembers.

Take the time to drink your tea
And look deep in your companions' eyes.
For in the give and take of brief humanity
You find the greatest prize.

When we're on the road to the Heavens
Through the gates that hold no lock
We have our most joyous journey
Hand in His hand around the block.

Veteran's Day

It is Veteran's Day 2000
A time for Americans to recall
The service one special group performed
For the safety and good of all

From the time of the Minuteman
That fought when freedom was begun
In our 365 day of liberty each year
We set aside this one
To take a moment, to say a prayer
Or just to turn our thoughts to them
They shed their freedom and the citizen life
Only to come back ... "Who knows when"

They rolled on seas in ships, soared in the air
Or tramped the dust and the mud on land
They served, they suffered and sacrificed more
Than a civilian can understand
Fighting here or on a foreign shore
Where life seems measured in mere hours
They fought, they feared, they lived and died
For the precious freedom that is ours.

Now each time an American flag is hoisted here
Or ordered to far off lands
And each time it's folded with reverence, then
Gets placed in a widow's hands
Remember who won, protected and fought for
The honored colors ... red, white and blue
And know when it's raised, lowered, honored or preserved
The Veteran's spirit passes through.

Have You Got "It"

Were we to sit down at His table,
With Him there at our side.
Would we have the strength to face Him,
And not have the urge to hide,
Some misgiving we've mismanaged,
Or a deed too dreadful to call a sin?
In short, if judged on your life's full measure,
Is there proof enough to die with Him?

There is no room for sporadic Christianity,
In a world so filled with strife.
It's a living, not a hobby,
It's not just for Sundays, it's for life.
We can't just breathe God in on the inhale,
And forget Him on the "ex".
Half of your time in the world as we know it,
Will not get you to the next.

Do not "practice" your faith from time to time,
Live it every day.
The good that will remain is the work you've done,
Not just in the words you say.
Make it your mission, not just a vision,
Or a prized treasure on a shelf.
Take more pride in the honor God is calling you,
And less pride .... In yourself.

To the Light

When your midnights seem forever,
When hope is hard to find.
When gloom and despair seem beyond repair,
Lost in shadows of the mind.
You can kindle but one candle,
And focus your faith's sight,
Not in looking back at all the black,
But forward, to the light.

We see ourselves on troubled seas,
And think disaster must prevail.
When far we're tossed and all seems lost,
Is just when one brave soul sets sail.
A tiny boat is then a signal,
Of horizons shining bright.
Break from the crowd, don't dwell on clouds,
But go forward to the light.

Without this history we'd be strangers,
To each other and the Word.
We'd not give the Good Book a second look,
Living for ourselves and not assured,
Of life beyond tomorrow,
Of morning after night,
Of passing through the gate, keyed but on faith,
And living in His light.

Lonesome Bones

Swept by the wind,
Sheltered in the snow,
Beneath the soil,
Lonesome bones.

Breeze scatters my flowers across the snow,
I don't care where they may blow,
I'm sure, at church, they stole the show.
They do not help my lonesome bones.

Females formerly found at my side,
For the first days come by with thoughts to hide,
Then remember when they thought I lied.
They abandon lonesome bones.

Laborers in fall across me rake,
In winter, family evergreen blankets make,
Till I look the part of a green clambake.
They do not warm these lonesome bones.

The words upon a stone, a token,
Of all I've written, sung or spoken,
Like my bones I leave none broken.
The only glory of lonesome bones.

I lay here silent as rot's begun,
Worms eat my protein from brain to bum,
But cannot chew my calcium.
I'm left to keep my lonesome bones.

As weeks go by I hear fewer feet,
Except for Cal, and sometimes Pete,
They come, remember, then retreat.
Uplifting thoughts for lonesome bones.

I sense some others joining me,
From side to side, but cannot see,
Who my next-door neighbors be.
Not important to lonesome bones.

I know my body was just on loan,
To enjoy life's colors, smells and tones,
Then make way for further Kelly's and Jones'.
Guess I'm grateful for my lonesome bones.

Elizabeth

The time of holding hands is done.
For a month, I haven't seen your smile.
You've vanished from my dreams at night,
For what seems a long, long while.

My flirtatious talk is silenced now
That you're "Hi There" is no more.
Your favorite ice cream remains upon the shelf
When I leave the grocery store.
My heart is simply split in two
And hurts like it's never hurt before.

I think of you in solitude,
Both on my part and on yours.
I'm guilty of leaving you behind, again,
When finishing my cemetery tours.

You parted several partnerships,
On the stand, you seemed so all alone.
You were private in your thoughts that day,
As I slowly drove you home.
How could someone so lovely and loving
Have such a somber tone?

You were circled by men who loved you
When we laid you down to rest.
Why was it, from all who entered your life,
Cancer stayed with you and loved you best.

I never shared my name with you.
I never shared your bed.
But I could not have been closer,
Then if we had been wed.
I was the last man that ever kissed you,
And stroked the hair upon your head.

I'm happy not being your guy for the moment,
But being the man in your life, instead.
It's said that trust is the highest honor,
That you give to one, what you hold most dear.
I cherish your trust in me love,
As your son lives with me here.

The Apron

It is a tradition in our small family,
With others, or alone,
To set the table with fine china,
And serve Sunday dinner in our home.
Whether to celebrate the autumn,
Or chase away the winter blahs,
There'd be a roast cooking in the oven,
And fresh flowers in a vase.

I'd do most of the cooking,
'Cause I really didn't mind.
Cal would do the entertaining,
As I cleaned the dishes left behind.
Betsy asked for oldies on the stereo,
And sip an after dinner drink.
Occasionally she'd come out and visit,
What she called "the maid out at the sink".

One week, at suppertime's conclusion,
Just as clean-up had begun,
Bets came out to the kitchen,
And stated there was an errand she had to run.
"Is there anything you needed?"
I said "No, the tea will be waiting for you here."
Betsy told me the service was so good today,
She'd bring back an apron for me to wear.

I had just gotten down to the pots and pans,
As Bets came back inside.
"I couldn't find my lacy one,
But this one's pretty" she beamed with pride.
"I'd like to help you put it on"
Smiling all the time, she said,
"Put the pan down on the counter",
Then she slipped it over my head.

I silently watched her laughing eyes,
And her bright red smiling lips,
As she smoothed the soft material down,
And tied it at my hips.
"We'll have our tea now, in the living room,"
As she walked away to join my wife.
I could just barely hold my laughter in,
Enjoying the embarrassment of my life.

Just we three were in the house that day,
So it really didn't matter.
I did just as she instructed,
And served dessert up on a platter.
I turned to go back to the kitchen,
My wife asked, "Leaving us so soon?
At least you could wiggle a little for us,
When you go to leave the room."

I shortened my step and rolled my hips,
Swaying out the door,
Leaving both my girlfriends laughing,
When I went out to finish the chores.
I removed the apron from my waist,
And folded it as neatly as it had been.
Betsy seemed disappointed with it off,
I smiled "maybe I'll wear it for you again."

When she left, I gave her a little curtsey,
In return, she took a little bow,
I recall the day with mixed emotions,
As I have neither of them now.
'Betsy's apron' is all that need be said,
Between my wife and I these days,
And she'll know I'm off to visit Betsy,
With a couple flowers from the vase.

A Hole in a Heart

I wish I could be happy,
I've got every right to be.
I have a steady job with good pay,
And a loving family.
I've excellent health and strong teeth,
I have three cars in the drive,
And decent food at every mealtime,
But I just don't feel alive.

As if I'm going through the motions,
Up at five most every day,
Coffee breakfast, beer at lunchtime,
By eleven, in the hay.
But there is surely something missing,
At work, in life or in my home,
For someone so blessed and privileged,
To feel so all alone.

My skies were never bluer,
The hills, a grateful green.
I know they're public, not possessions,
Just for my eyes to be seeing.
I love heights and stormy weather,
I'm at home with a gentle breeze,
I don't care for crowded parties,
As much as the company of trees.

I don't shirk responsibilities,
My obligations I don't fight,
But the balance of these set on me,
Don't seem to add up right.
Nature asks little in the contest,
Just respect and let it be.
Why can't people be more natural,
In what they want from me?

I'll not go up to the mountains,
And live there every day,
Nor choose a tropic island,
And like a hermit, stay.
I'll continue what I'm doing,
In calm or crashing weather,
To remain loyal to human beings,
And ignore the others all together.

I wish I could be happy,
But that wish, I feel, I'm losing.

Don't Linger Long

Too late, my dear,
The time has come,
To set a broken heart.
And too, I fear,
My time is done,
As we must truly part.

If spirits may
Come back to earth,
Well past the time for tears,
I will, and stay,
For all it's worth,
And lightly whisper for just your ears.

Don't linger long
Among the grass,
That marks a day of reckoning.
Instead, grow strong,
Drink from life's glass,
Not of our reunions beckoning.

One must stay
And the other fly,
One to lie down, the other stand.
Until the day
Of no goodbyes,
May God cradle you in His hand.

Tribute to a Friend

There is a special kind of friendship,
That some don't have, or cannot reach,
Of the smiling openheartedness,
From both ends of a leash.
"Mans best friend"? it fails to cover,
The bond between owner and a pet,
From the day you pick your buddy up,
From the pound or from the vet.

He may eat you out of house and home.
He may wet your floors as a little pup,
But when you have a down day at work,
He's always home to pick you up.
Yeah, there's times he eats your basement,
Or somehow get bleach on his butt and tail,
But the next day he's bounding at your feet,
As you go out to get the mail.

You'd do anything for your good old dog,
Just as for your kids or for your wife.
He'd protect the family till his final breath.
It's more than just a "dogs life".
So, goodbye my good four footed partner,
Thanks for taking such good care of me.
I'll do the same for you by taking you out,
To the shade of your favorite tree.

The Garden

"Come and see my garden"
Smiling at the half opened door.
"I know that you've seen some of it
but I want to show you more".
Her hand, outstretched and tender
A soft twinkle in her eye
The gentle breeze of her voice calling, was
Too much to be denied.

I was led along the garden path
The setting sun filtering through the trees
Lavender scent released to the heavens
as she brushed it with her knees.
We approached a bed of roses
The sun circling her head like a crown
She lowered herself to the old oak bench
and bade me to sit down.

"Gaze upon my fresh new roses
Hold the petals, stroke the leaves
Breathe deeply of their perfume
For that's what my garden needs.
Look closely at the rosebuds,
Not yet ready to burst in flower
Holding back it's showy moment
Until the proper hour".

My fingers traced the unopened bloom
And felt its silky shell
Slightly damp with the coming dew

That an evening garden knows so well.
My companion nodded appreciation
Of my gentleness toward her treasure
And laid her head down on my shoulder
In an expression of her pleasure.

"You're the only person I've shown this to
Or allowed to touch it with their hand
I'd like you to see the garden darken
Please, stay a while longer if you can".
So we strolled the path by moonlight
In the early evening hours.
An arm around each others waist
Looking closer at her flowers.

She stopped and picked a fragrant one
"A gardenia for my friend"
The took two pink carnations
And intertwined them at the ends.
"I'd like you to wear this for me,
call it a joining of the soul"
She kissed me softly on the cheek
Slipping the stems through a button hole.

"No one else need ever know of this
It's just between you and me,
I'm sure the moon won't breathe a word
and no one else can see".
She stroked the lovely flowers
and sent a shiver through my heart.
"I hope the closeness in this moment
·Will ensure we never part".

"I guess I better let you go now
It's getting rather late".
The fragrance of her floral art went with me
As she closed the garden gate.
In later days the plot went to weeds
The house is now dark and bare
My love has moved away, as well
But the memory is always there.

Printed in the United States
by Baker & Taylor Publisher Services